GEO

FRIENDS
OF ACPL

5/06 P9-CND-508

Cheerleading

Cheer Skills

Beginning Tumbling and Stunting

by Jen Jones

Capstone press

Mankato, Minnesota

Snap Books are published by Capstone Press,
151 Good Counsel Drive, P.O. Box 669, Mankato, Minnesota 56002
www.capstonepress.com

Copyright © 2006 by Capstone Press. All rights reserved.
No part of this publication may be reproduced in whole or in part, or stored
in a retrieval system, or transmitted in any form or by any means,
electronic, mechanical, photocopying, recording, or otherwise, without
written permission of the publisher.
For information regarding permission, write to Capstone Press,
151 Good Counsel Drive, P.O. Box 669, Dept. R, Mankato, Minnesota 56002.
Printed in the United States of America

Library of Congress Cataloging-in-Publication Data
Jones, Jen, 1976-
   Cheer skills: beginning tumbling and stunting / by Jen Jones.
      p. cm. — (Snap books cheerleading)
   Includes index.
   ISBN 0-7368-4358-2 (hardcover)
   1. Cheerleading — Juvenile literature. I. Title. II. Series.
   LB3635.J633 2006
   791.6'4 — dc22   2005007267

Summary: A guide for children and pre-teens on cheerleading exercises,
moves, and stunts.

Editor: Deb Berry/Bill SMITH STUDIO
Illustrators: Lisa Parett; Roxanne Daner, Marina Terletsky and Brock Waldron/Bill SMITH STUDIO
Designers: Marina Terletsky, and Brock Waldron/Bill SMITH STUDIO
Photo Researcher: Iris Wong/Bill SMITH STUDIO

Photo Credits: Cover: Tony Anderson/Getty Images; 10, Olivier Ribardiere/Getty Images;
13, Dennis MacDonald/Alamy; 16, Getty Images; 26, Logan Wallace/Syracuse Newspapers/The Image Works;
32, Britton Lenahan. Back Cover, Getty Images. All other photos by Tim Jackson Photography.

1 2 3 4 5 6 10 09 08 07 06 05

Table of Contents

I Can Fly, I Can Fly, I Can Fly

Cheerleaders are lucky. Like flying circus performers, they can make an audience's spirit soar while soaring through the air. Cheer tumbling and stunting are the stuff that "oohs" and "aahs" are made of. They are exciting to watch and challenging to perform. Stunting calls for serious teamwork, and tumbling demands top endurance. In other words, cheerleaders are truly amazing athletes.

4

"Cheerleaders are truly amazing athletes."

In **competition** cheerleading, "basket tosses," flips, and partner stunts are all in a day's work. Some **squads** will even perform full twists, "scorpions," and "liberty heel" stretches. Though these skills can't be learned overnight, it is possible with patience, trust, and attention to safety.

In this book, you'll learn beginning stunts and tumbling. We'll build a solid ground for doing tougher tricks in the future. It's important to get the simple stuff down before you can move on to the really big stunts.

See you on the "flip" side!

REMEMBER! SAFETY FIRST!

5

Getting Started with A Winning Approach

Cheer teams fit into two categories. "Building" teams stunt and tumble, while "non-building" teams only tumble. No matter which style of team you're on, it's smart to learn all of the skills described in this book. Not only do they make you a more well-rounded athlete, but they also make you better prepared for high school and college cheering in the future.

Throughout the book, you'll learn

▶ Proper stretching and **conditioning** techniques

▶ Exercises for increased power and strength

▶ **Mounts** and tumbling skills

▶ How to get over your fears

Cheerleading has come a long way since the "pony mounts" and "pyramids" of the past. You'll develop strength and endurance while learning the principles of teamwork and trust.

Although this book provides instruction, it is not meant to be used in place of regular gymnastics classes and stunting training. Always practice with a trained teacher or cheer coach. Now let the learning begin.

Smart Stretches

It's all about conditioning. (No, not for shiny hair.) Cheer conditioning means stretching and working out often to get your body in tip-top athletic shape. Without proper stretching before games and practices, you won't be able to move as well. You'll also be more likely to get hurt. No smart cheerleader wants to take that risk.

Stretching doesn't have to be a chore. Make it fun by playing dance music. These stretches are sure to give you a great warm-up.

◀ Butterfly

Sitting cross-legged, touch the soles of your feet together. Holding your ankles, use your elbows to push the knees toward the ground. Hold for ten seconds, then "flutter" the knees to shake it out. Repeat.

Bridge ▶

Lying on your back, hands should be on the ground close to your head with elbows in the air. Press your body upward while straightening your arms and legs. Your stomach and hips should be highest in the air, with your body arched in an upside-down "U" shape.

9

Cheer-Gymnastics For Newbies

Cartwheels and round-offs seem like kids' stuff, but these simple tricks are the building blocks of gymnastics. Before you can tumble like Carly Patterson, you need to learn the simpler moves.

3 1833 04649 7530

Just for Kicks
Perfect Cartwheels

Ready to make like a windmill? Stand with left foot in front, your body turned right. Lift right leg as left hand touches the ground. Next, right hand touches down as left leg goes into the air. (Your body looks like an "X" at the midpoint.) Keep your body straight and point your toes. As feet land in lunge position, raise hands above head.

You Spin Me Round
Rockin' Round-Offs

Round-offs are like more powerful cartwheels. They use power to push your body into handsprings and flips. Prep and execution are similar to the cartwheel, though you may take a running start.

Round-offs differ from cartwheels in these ways.

* Your body is in handspring position at midpoint.

* Your feet land together.

* Your body faces backwards when finished.

Stunting for Starters

> It may take two to dance, but it takes three to build a successful partner stunt.

The flyer is the person on top of a stunt. Must have balance, flexibility, courage.

The base lifts the flyer in the air and supports her weight. Must have strength and patience.

The spotter watches stunts to ensure safety. If a stunt looks shaky or falls, the spotter steps in to save the day. Spotters must have safety knowledge and must pay attention.

 Flyer

Your coach decides whether you will be a flyer, base, or spotter based on your weight, strength, height, and ability.

The thigh stand is an easy, safe stunt for beginners.

Base Stand in lunge position (one leg bent, the other leg straight) facing forward. When the flyer steps onto your thigh, hold her knees as support.

Flyer With hands on base's shoulders, step onto base's thigh. Lock your legs as she takes hold of your knees. Once steady, hit an arm motion.

Bases

Gymnastics that Dazzle

Once you're turning cartwheels and round-offs like a champ, it's time to move on to the big leagues. Remember that mid-level and advanced skills should never be attempted without a gymnastics coach, trained spotter, or cheer coach present. Otherwise, you may seriously hurt yourself or others and not be able to cheer. Got it? Let's get to learning!

The best gymnasts know that there are three secrets to great tumbling.

Technique involves correctly doing the skill from prep to finish. It also means paying attention to detail like pointed toes, straight legs, and clean **rotations**.

Balance is evenly keeping your body weight and staying in the right position while tumbling. To improve balance, try the "Eagle Sit." Sitting cross-legged, grab your ankles with your hands. Extend legs in a "V" and hold for five seconds.

Body Control is just that, keeping control as you flip and twist. You can improve body control by doing some of the strengthening exercises described later in the book.

If you're already dreaming of flying through the air, that's great. Working toward advanced skills will make you a determined gymnast. To work up to the fancy stuff, you must first learn walkovers and handsprings. From there, you'll move on to tucks, flips, and aerials. Now, get ready for greatness.

Back Walkovers

A back walkover uses the **bridge** described earlier and is good prep for learning the back handspring.

1. Stand with feet close together and hands overhead.

2. Bend body backwards into "bridge" position.

3. Kick legs over, landing one at a time.

4. Stand straight up with arms overhead.

Back Handsprings

Ready to put some "spring" in your step? Handsprings are often done after round-offs to gather steam. Best learned on a trampoline or incline mat, they should only be attempted with a trained spotter.

1. Starting with arms raised, swing them down behind you and bend your knees.

2. Throw hands back over your head and spring backward with legs. This motion should push you into a handstand position.

3. Push off the ground and snap feet back into standing position.

Flying High

The thigh stand, learned earlier, plays an important role because many stunts naturally progress from it.

Begin the following stunts in thigh stand position.

L-Stand

Base Holding flyer's outer leg, grasp lifted leg at ankle. For dismount, guide lifted leg forward and catch at waist as flyer jumps down.

Flyer Raise inner leg above base's head. Hit an "L" motion with arms. For dismount, bring lifted leg forward and land with feet together.

Shoulder Sit

Base Go from lunge to standing position after flyer sits on shoulders. Hold flyer's thighs. For dismount, bring hands inside flyer's legs, grasp her hands briefly and bend as she jumps to the ground.

Flyer Swing inner leg around base's shoulders while keeping outer leg straight. Hit a "High V" once situated on shoulders. For dismount, grasp base's hands and jump to the ground behind base.

For each stunt, spotter should support and catch at the waist if needed.

From this point, you have nowhere to go but up.

An "elevator to shoulders" is a more advanced stunt that should only be attempted after you feel comfortable in your stunting ability.

Elevator to Shoulders

Bases Facing each other, squat with hands cupped in front of you. Dip as flyer lands in your hands, then shrug upward, lifting flyer to shoulder level. For dismount, join hands with flyer and catch under her arm as she jumps to ground.

Flyer Put your hands on bases' shoulders and step or jump into their hands, depending on skill level. (You can work up to jumping as you become more advanced.) Feet should be no more than shoulder width apart. As bases straighten, push off their shoulders to stand and hit a "High V" at the top.

Spotter While the flyer is loading into bases' hands, support at waist. Spotter then helps lift flyer and supports flyer at calves or knees. At landing, spotter supports the flyer's wrists.

"You have nowhere to go but up!"

Safety and Strengthening, Tumbling

Conditioning is a big part of safe tumbling and helps you pack a more powerful punch. Studies show that the areas used most in tumbling are the shoulders, arms, quadriceps and hamstrings (in your legs). To go from bony to buff, check out these proven exercises tailor-made for those body parts.

22

Hamstrings

Back Leg Lifts Lay on the ground face down with legs straight. Starting with right leg, do ten lifts upward keeping your toes pointed. Repeat with left leg.

Quadriceps

Balancing Act In a standing position, lift one foot and bend leg behind you. Keep knees close together and grab foot while in the air. Hold pose as long as you can. Repeat with other leg.

Shoulders

Partner Pull One cheerleader sits on the floor with legs straight in front of her and arms extended behind her parallel to the floor. Her partner grasps her wrists and pulls upward and inward gently for the stretch.

Safety and Strengthening, Stunting

Talk about heavy lifting! Cheerleaders lift, toss, and support their teammates, who are often the same weight. As a base or flyer, serious strength is needed for safe lifting and dismounting. When conditioning, pay special attention to the arms, shoulders, lower back, abdominals, and quadriceps.

Awesome Arch (Lower Back)

Lie face down with arms behind head and legs straight. All at once, lift head, arms, chest, feet and legs. Hold arch for five seconds and lower slowly. Repeat.

Da Dip (Upper Arms)

Bend legs with feet on the ground. Place hands behind you with fingers pointing toward your body. Lift hips into the air. Dip hips and bottom toward the ground as you bend your elbows, then push back up to lifted position. Repeat ten times.

Ready for Lift-Off (Quadriceps)

Squat with hands on the floor. Jump back to push-up position and quickly return to squat. Now jump as high as you can. Land in squat position and repeat.

Fear Factor

In the words of President Franklin D. Roosevelt, "The only thing to fear is fear itself." Sure, you're thinking, but did he ever say that from the top of a liberty or before throwing a back tuck? That's a good point!

It's totally normal to be afraid at first, but with proper attention to safety and *technique*, there is little reason to worry. Check out these ideas for facing your fears.

REMEMBER! SAFETY FIRST!

Star in your own movie

Athletes and performers have learned that if you can picture yourself doing something successfully, you're more likely to do so. Set aside quiet time to picture yourself performing a tough skill, then imagine it again right before attempting it. Lights, camera, action!

Learn how to trust

Everyone relies on each other for safety, so trust is needed between teammates. If not, you may tense up during a tumbling run or stunt, putting yourself and others in danger.

Team-Building Time

Stunting asks cheerleaders to put their well-being in someone else's hands. To do so willingly and without fear demands tremendous teamwork. The following are fun exercises that can build trust between cheerleaders.

Chain Gang Everyone should line up with ankles touching her neighbors' ankles. From this point, feet are glued together until further notice. (It's like a three-legged race, only with the whole squad.) The line then tries to cross the finish line as a group. This is a great activity for really making you feel like a team.

Operation Interaction Turn practice into a squad retreat, or if you're really gung-ho, go for a sleepover. Your coach can plan some icebreakers and goal-setting sessions for maximum bonding.

Guiding Lights Set up a winding course with parking cones, limbo sticks, chairs, or tires. Everyone teams up with one person wearing a blindfold as the other guides her through the course. Your trust will skyrocket after this exercise.

GLOSSARY

abdominals (ab-DOM-uh-nulz) the muscles of your belly, called "abs" for short

competition (kom-puh-TISH-uhn) a contest between two or more people trying to win the same thing

conditioning (kuhn-DISH-uhn-ing) working out and stretching to get your body in shape

dismount (diss-MOUNT) to get down from a cheer stunt

hamstrings (HAM-stringz) muscles in the back of your thighs

mount (MOUNT) to get on top of a stunt

quadriceps (KWAHD-ruh-seps) muscles in the front of your thighs

rotation (roh-TAY-shuhn) to turn in a circle, such as in a cheer stunt

squad (SKWAHD) a team of cheerleaders

technique (tek-NEEK) the way in which you do something, such as performing a cheer stunt

FAST FACTS

Some college squads are famous for special stunts they have made up.

"Diamond Head"
Kansas State University

The squad first performed this diamond-shaped stunt in 1983 and often does a full turn while in the shape.

"Wolf Wall"
North Carolina State University

It takes 14 people to pull off this stunt. Named for the "NC State Wolfpack," the stunt looks like a wall and is very difficult.

READ MORE

Ferralli, Mike. *A Guide to Beginner Tumbling*. Baltimore, Maryland: American Literary Press, 2003.

McElroy, James T. *We've Got Spirit: The Life and Times of America's Greatest Cheerleading Team*. New York: Berkley Publishing Group, 2000.

Peters, Craig. *Competitive Cheerleading*. Broomall, Pennsylvania: Mason Crest, 2003.

Wilson, Leslie. *The Ultimate Guide to Cheerleading*. New York: Three Rivers Press, 2003.

INTERNET SITES

 **FactHound** offers a safe, fun way to find Internet sites related to this book. All of the sites on FactHound have been researched by our staff.

Here's how

1. Visit *www.facthound.com*

2. Type in this special code **0736843582** for age-appropriate sites. Or enter a search word related to this book for a more general search.

3. Click on the **Fetch It** button. FactHound will fetch the best sites for you!

ABOUT THE AUTHOR

While growing up in Ohio, Jen Jones spent seven years as a cheerleader for her grade school and high school squads. Following high school, she coached several cheer squads to team victory. For two years, she also cheered and created dance numbers for the Chicago Lawmen semi-professional football dance team.

Jen gets her love of cheerleading honestly, because her mother, sister, and cousins are also heavily involved in the sport. As well as teaching occasional dance and cheerleading workshops, Jen now works in sunny Los Angeles as a freelance writer for publications like *American Cheerleader* and *Dance Spirit*.

Index